Let's Do It!

I Talk You Talk Press

CONTENTS

CHAPTER ONE

Mike drove into the office car park and parked his car. He got out of his car and got into his wheelchair. He wheeled over to the front entrance of Sunrise. Dean was sitting in his wheelchair in front of the building. He was talking to Jonathan. Jonathan was standing next to Dean.

"Good morning," said Mike. "What are you both doing outside? It's cold today."

Dean looked at the office entrance door and then at Mike.

"A man from the government is here," he said quietly.

"Really? What does he want?" asked Mike.

"I don't know," said Dean. "But there is a meeting at nine o'clock."

"Maybe he wants to give us more work," said Mike.

"I don't think so," said Jonathan. "I think it will be bad news."

Mike smiled. "You always think things are bad," he said.

"That's because most things are bad," said Jonathan.

"Come on, let's go inside," said Mike. "We have work to do."

The three men went up the ramp and into the small office building.

There was a man from the government standing by the window. He was looking at some documents in a file.

The other workers started to arrive. Abeni walked into the office.

"Good morning!" she said brightly. Then she saw the man from the government. She walked over to Mike. "Why is he here?" she asked quietly.

"I don't know," said Mike. "But we have a meeting at nine."

Mike sat at his desk and turned on his computer. He looked at the time. It was 8:50am.

I have a lot of work to do, he thought. *But I'll wait until the meeting has finished.*

At 9:00am, the man from the government said, "Good morning, everyone. I have something to tell you." He stood at the front of the office. The ten workers in the room sat and listened to the man.

"The government opened this office, Sunrise, ten years ago. We needed people to enter data into our system. We thought it was a good job for people with disabilities. It has been a great success. You have all worked very hard. You do a good job with the work that we send you. You are always very fast and accurate. I'd like to thank you for doing a good job. But times have changed. The economic situation in the town is not good. The local government doesn't have much money.

"This building needs upgrading. It will be expensive. We were worrying about this. Then a large company in another city came to see us. They say they can do all the work that you do for the same amount of money, and we won't have to fix this building. So, I'm very sorry, but we are going to close this office."

"What?"

"Close this office?"

"What about our jobs?"

Everyone started asking questions. They looked at each other. They were shocked.

"What are we going to do?" asked Mike. "We have disabilities. It will be difficult for us to find other jobs."

"I don't think so," said the man. "You are good workers. I'm sure other companies will want to hire you."

"But very few companies have a barrier-free environment," said Dean. "Our work options are limited."

"You will find new jobs. I'm sure," said the man.

"When will the office close?" asked Abeni.

"Next month," said the man.

"Next month?! That's so soon!" shouted Jill. "You can't do this to us! I can't work anywhere else. Sometimes I am too depressed to come to work. Other companies won't hire me."

"I'm sure they will hire you," said the man. "I'm sorry, but that is the situation. Good luck in finding new jobs."

Everyone watched him walk out of the office.

When the man had gone, everyone started talking.

"They can't do this to us."

"What are we going to do?"

"I'll never find a new job."

"OK, OK," said Mike. "Listen everybody. We have to stop the government. We need to keep this office open. Let's make a plan."

Everyone listened.

"We can have demonstrations. We can ask our families and friends to come and stand outside the office. We can tell people in the community. We can call the local newspaper and TV station."

"That's a good idea," said Jonathan. "But I don't want to be on TV."

"OK, you don't have to be on TV. When the TV cameras arrive, you can come inside the office," said Mike.

"Let's start planning the demonstration," said Dean. "When is the best time for it?"

"How about next Saturday? Our friends and families work during the week. Weekends are best," said Mike.

"OK. Let's make some signs," said Abeni. "I can make a nice design."

"Yes, you are very creative," said Mike.

"What are we going to write on the signs?" asked Greg.

"Let's write, 'Save our jobs!'" said Abeni.

"Good idea," said Dean. "Let's start planning the demonstration details now. I don't feel like working today."

"No," said Mike. "We are paid to work. We must finish our work, and then we can plan. Who can stay late today?"

CHAPTER TWO

The next Saturday, the workers and their friends and families were outside the office.

There were around thirty people. A local newspaper reporter, and a TV station crew were there too.

Everyone held signs, and shouted, "Save our jobs!"

The TV reporter was talking to Mike.

"Can you tell me more details?" asked the reporter. The cameraman came and filmed Mike.

"Sure," said Mike. "All the workers here have disabilities. We have been working here for ten years. The government wants to close the office. They want to save money. They plan to give our work to a big company in another city. We have to find jobs in other companies. But it will be difficult for us. We need this office. We need our jobs."

The thirty people stayed outside the office for around two hours. The road next to the office was busy. There were many cars. Many people slowed down to look at the people.

On Monday, some people came to the office. They said, "We saw you on TV. It's very bad news. We will call the government. We will try to stop them closing your office."

Many people called the government. The workers and their friends and families had another demonstration the next Saturday. But it was no good. The government did not change its plan.

On the last day of work, Mike said to everyone, "It's our last day. I have an idea. Everyone listen."

Everyone stopped working and moved towards Mike.

"We all tried to find new jobs. But no one was interested in us. We will have trouble finding new jobs," he said. "So, I have been thinking. Why don't we start our own business?"

Everyone looked at Mike.

"Our own business? What kind of business?" asked Jonathan.

"How about a design and printing business?" said Mike. "We can get a loan from the bank, buy some equipment, and get work from local companies. What do you think?"

Everyone was quiet for a few seconds. Then, Dean said, "I think it's a great idea. I want to do it."

"I want to do it, too," said Abeni. "I have an online degree in graphic design."

"That's why you are good at design," said Mike. "If we do it, we will need you."

"I want to join too," said Jonathan.

"Me too," said Greg. "I have qualifications in maths."

"Yes, you are great with numbers Greg. You can help to write the business plan," said Mike. "Does anyone else want to join?"

The other five workers shook their heads.

"I'm going to rest for a few months," said Ralph. "Then, I'm going to work for my brother. He has a business in the next town."

"It's a good idea," said Jill. "But a new business means stress. And stress is not good for me."

"My parents stayed in this town because I had a job. Now I have no job, so they plan to move to the countryside. I will go with them," said Leo.

Aman and Susan said, "We will go to the job centre and keep looking for new jobs."

"I see," said Mike. "So it's me, Dean, Jonathan, Greg and Abeni. Five of us."

"Yes! Let's do it!" said Dean.

"This is a great idea! It's so exciting!" said Abeni. "What are we going to call the company?"

"Any ideas?" asked Mike.

Abeni thought for a few seconds. Then, she said, "How about Artistic Design and Printing? ADAP….adaptable!"

"Good idea! I like it!" said Dean.

"And who is going to be the boss?" asked Abeni.

Everyone was quiet for a few seconds, then Dean said, "I think

Mike should be the boss. He's a good leader."

"I agree," said Abeni.

"I agree too," said Jonathan.

"So do I," said Greg.

Mike smiled. "OK, I'll be the boss. But don't worry, I'll be a nice boss!"

Everyone laughed.

"But wait," said Greg. "We need to write a business plan. Then, we need to go to the bank to get a loan. Then, we need to find a building. We have no office. We have nothing. Tomorrow, we won't see each other. How are we going to plan our business?"

"We can meet in Julie's café in the centre of town," said Mike. "We can have our meetings there. Julie won't mind."

"What about rival companies?" asked Jonathan.

"There is only one other design and printing company in the town," said Mike. "I checked online last night. It's Harper's Design and Printing. It's a family business. Two brothers run it."

"They might be angry if we start a rival company," said Jonathan.

"Yes, they might be angry. But we are free to start our own company," said Mike. "OK. Let's start planning!"

CHAPTER THREE

The five friends spent the next few weeks making their business plan. They met in Julie's café every day. Julie gave them free coffee and free lunches.

"I think the government's actions are terrible," she said. "I will help you as much as I can."

She also read their business plan and gave them advice.

"OK," said Mike one day. "I think the plan is ready to take to a bank. We need to borrow fifteen thousand pounds. We need to rent a small building and buy the printing equipment. We can use our own computers, but we need to buy design software."

"Should we find a building first?" asked Abeni.

Julie was listening. "I think that's a good idea," she said. "My friend owns a rental company. I'll call her and ask her to help you find a building."

"Thank you, Julie, that's a great help," said Mike. "We need a building which has wheelchair access, and is barrier-free. And somewhere that is not too expensive."

"I'll call my friend now," said Julie. "She's the owner of 'King Estates'. Do you know it?"

"I've heard of it," said Dean. "It's on the other side of town, isn't it?"

"Yes," said Julie. "But she handles buildings all over the town."

Julie went into the kitchen to call her friend.

"I hope King Estates has a good building," said Jonathan. "And we need good security. Cameras. We need security cameras."

Mike smiled. "I don't think we will have much trouble."

"No," said Jonathan. "Maybe not. But I'll feel better if we have cameras."

"OK, we will get cameras," said Mike.

Julie came back. "My friend will come here this afternoon. She will introduce you to some buildings," she said.

"Thank you, Julie, that's great," said Mike.

Later that afternoon, Julie's friend, Fatima, came to the café.

"I think the government is wrong. I want to help you," she said. She sat down and opened up her computer. "I have some buildings which might be OK. Some don't have a ramp outside for wheelchairs, but we can add a ramp."

They all looked at the buildings on Fatima's website.

"They are expensive," said Greg.

"Yes, office buildings are expensive," said Fatima.

"How about this one?" said Dean. He pointed to a small building.

"It isn't an office," said Fatima. "It's a house. Actually, a person in a wheelchair used to live there. So it might be OK for you."

"We can make it into an office. We don't need much space, and this is cheap," said Dean.

Everyone looked at the photographs of the house. There were no other buildings near it.

"It's outside the town centre," said Fatima. "Do you drive?"

"Of course we do," said Mike.

"OK, I'll contact the owner of the house and tell him you are interested in it," said Fatima.

She picked up her phone and called the owner. She spoke to him for a few minutes. Then, she said, "The owner is interested in renting the house to you. Would you like to see it? You can look at it today."

"Great. Let's go today," said Mike.

An hour later, the five friends, the owner and Fatima were standing in the house. It was a very small house. It was perfect. They looked around the living room.

"We can put desks in the middle of the room, and the printing equipment near the window," said Dean. "We need to buy a ramp for the entrance too."

"The last tenant was in a wheelchair. He brought his own ramp.

He took it when he left here. But I'll buy the ramp," said the owner. "I want to help you. But first, you have to get a loan from the bank."

"Yes," said Mike. "That's the difficult part! I'll go to the bank tomorrow."

"I hope they will lend us the money," said Jonathan. "If they don't, what are we going to do?"

"Don't worry," said Mike. "I'm sure they will want to help us."

CHAPTER FOUR

The next day, Mike put his suit on. He hadn't worn it for a long time. He sat on his bed and looked at himself in the mirror.

I look smart, he thought. *This is an important day. I have to look my best.*

Mike used to be a good sportsman. He played tennis, and badminton. He worked in a busy office. He wore a suit every day. But ten years ago, he had a car accident. His legs were damaged. He couldn't walk. He had been using a wheelchair since then. At first, Mike was angry and upset. But now, he was used to his new life. He just had one wish. He wanted a girlfriend. It was difficult to find a girlfriend when he was in a wheelchair.

I should stop thinking about that. This business is more important, he thought.

He picked up his briefcase and put the business plan in it. He pulled himself into his wheelchair and left his house. He got in his car and drove into the town centre.

Which bank should I try? he thought. *I'll try First Bank. It's the nearest to the car park.* He parked his car in the big car park and got into his wheelchair. Mike played wheelchair basketball and raced in wheelchair marathons. His wheelchair was small and light because his arms were strong. *I'm lucky,* he thought. *Dean's wheelchair is electric. It's big and heavy. It's more difficult for him.*

He got to the bank and went in.

He saw a man sitting at a desk. The sign on the desk said, --- 'Loans'---.

This is the person I need to talk to, he thought. He went to the desk.

The man looked up.

"Good morning, sir," he said. "How can I help you?"

"I'd like to talk about getting a loan to start a business," said Mike.

The man looked at Mike and then at his wheelchair.

"Oh, OK," he said. He stood up and walked to the other side of the desk. He moved the chair. "Please," he said to Mike.

Mike moved to the desk.

"What kind of business do you want to start?" asked the man.

"A design and printing business," said Mike. "We have a business plan." He took the business plan out of his briefcase and passed it to the man.

"Thank you," said the man. Mike watched him while he read the business plan.

I hope he says yes, thought Mike. *He should do. The numbers are good. The plan is very detailed.*

After around ten minutes, the man looked up. "It's a good business plan," he said. "But there is one problem. You don't have any customers."

"We will get customers after we start the business," said Mike.

"And how are you going to get customers?"

"We are going to go to every business in the town," said Mike.

The man looked at Mike's wheelchair again. "I see," he said. "I don't want to be rude, but...well...are the other members of your company in wheelchairs?"

"One other member is in a wheelchair. Two have mental disabilities. One has Asperger's Syndrome. But that doesn't affect our work. We all worked for Sunrise, the office for people with disabilities," said Mike.

"Ah, yes, it closed, didn't it?" said the man.

"Yes. But we all worked very hard. It was a success. And our new business will be a success, too," said Mike.

The man looked at the business plan again. "You want fifteen thousand pounds," he said. "That's a lot of money."

"Yes, I know. But as the business plan says, we need to pay rent for the building, buy equipment and make marketing materials. We also need to pay ourselves a little until we start making money."

The man was quiet for a few minutes.

What is he thinking? thought Mike. *I hope he says yes.*

"I'm sorry if this is a rude question," said the man. "But do you take a lot of time off to go to hospitals?"

"We all go to hospitals, but not so often. Some members go once a week, others go once a month. I go every three months."

"Hmm…" said the man. He looked at his computer, then he looked at the business plan, and then at Mike.

"I'm sorry. I think it will be a risk to lend you the money. You have no customers, and…"

"And what? We are disabled?" Mike was angry. "It doesn't affect our ability to work."

"No, no," said the man. "I didn't mean that. But…I'm sorry."

Mike took the business plan and put it in his briefcase. "It's OK. I understand," he said. He was angry.

"Thank you for your time."

He went away from the desk and wheeled out of the bank.

He didn't want to give us the money because we have disabilities, he thought. *He doesn't trust our ability to work. Well, we don't want this bank's money. I'll try a different bank.*

CHAPTER FIVE

Mike sat outside the Govern Bank and looked up at the entrance. There were many steps, but no ramp.

I can't get into this bank! he thought. *They don't think about people in wheelchairs. This is not a good bank for me. But there is only one more bank in the town. Switch Bank. I will try them.*

The bank was on the other side of town. It took Mike thirty minutes to get there. When he arrived, a woman was waiting by the door.

"Good morning, sir," she said.

"Good morning," he said to her. "I'd like to talk to someone about getting a business loan."

"A business loan? Sure. You can talk to Mr Singh. He's the loan manager. Please wait a moment," said the woman. She went to a room at the back of the bank.

Mike waited a few minutes, then the woman came back.

"Mr Singh will see you now," she said. "Please come this way."

Mike followed her into the room at the back of the bank.

A man was inside. He stood up when he saw Mike. "Good morning, sir," he said. "Please come in."

He shook Mike's hand and moved the chair next to the desk to make room for Mike's wheelchair.

"So, you want to start a business? That's good. We need more businesses in this town," he said. "Do you have any experience?"

"We don't have any experience running a business. But we all worked for Sunrise, so we have work experience.

"Ah, yes," said Mr Singh. "I saw the story on the news. The government closed the office. That was not right. Disabled people need jobs too."

"Yes," said Mike. "We all lost our jobs. So some of us decided to start our own business."

"Good," said Mr Singh. "Do you have a business plan?"

Mike took the business plan out of his briefcase and handed it to Mr Singh.

"Here you are," he said.

Mr Singh read the business plan. It took him around fifteen minutes.

"The numbers look good," he said. "Is one of your company members good with numbers?"

"Yes. That's Greg. He doesn't need to use a calculator. We call him the human calculator. He isn't so good at talking to people, but he is a genius with numbers," said Mike.

"That's good," said Mr Singh. "Every business needs someone who is good with numbers. I see that you have found an office."

"Yes, just a small one. It's a small house. But it's big enough for us."

"Good. And you are doing design and printing? Who is your designer?"

"That's Abeni. She has times when she is very creative. And she has a degree in graphic design."

"And how are you going to get customers?" asked Mr Singh.

"We are going to go to every business in the town," said Mike. "We are also going to make a website and get customers from other towns."

Mr Singh nodded. "I see. Well…" He thought for a few seconds.

"I think I should give you a chance," he said. "I'm going to lend you the money."

"Really? That's great!" said Mike. "Thank you so much!"

"You will need a bank account. You can set one up here, at our bank. Who is the manager of the business?"

"I am," said Mike.

"Good. You can do the paperwork now," said Mr Singh. He shook Mike's hand.

"Well done," he said. "And good luck."

Thirty minutes later, Mike left the bank. He was very happy. He sent a group message to the other members of the company.

---- *'We did it! We got a loan!'*---

Within a few seconds, he started to get messages from the other members.

---- *'That's great news! Well done!'*----

---- *'Yes! We should celebrate!'*----

Mike smiled. He looked up at the blue sky.

Today is a good day, he thought. *Now, I'll go and see Fatima. I'll tell her the good news and ask her when we can move into our new office.*

CHAPTER SIX

Two weeks later, Mike, Dean, Abeni, Jonathan and Greg were in their new office. The equipment had been delivered. Greg was setting up the computers and installing software. Abeni was drawing designs for the flyers and business cards. Mike and Dean were watching Jonathan.

Jonathan was standing on a desk in the corner of the room. He was putting a camera on the ceiling.

"I don't think we need cameras," said Dean. "No one is going to break in. We are just a small business with printing equipment and a few computers. And we are getting an alarm system. If anyone breaks in, the alarm will ring."

Jonathan looked at him. "Of course we need cameras," he said. "There are not many other people around this building. No one will hear the alarm. And I want to watch the office at nights."

"OK, that's fine," said Mike. "But that camera is really small. No one will see it."

"That's my plan," said Jonathan. "If someone breaks in, they will look for a camera. They won't see this one."

"Are you going to watch the office every night?" asked Dean.

"For the first few weeks, yes," said Jonathan.

"I don't think you need to watch it every night," said Dean.

"I think I do. I'm going to put a very small camera outside the front door, too," said Jonathan. "We will be safe with cameras."

Mike smiled. Jonathan was always talking about cameras.

He moved over to Abeni. He looked at her designs.

"They look great!" he said. *"Artistic Design and Printing. For all your design and printing needs.* I like it. It looks and sounds good."

"I'm going to design the flyer on the computer when Greg has finished installing the software," she said.

"Nearly finished," said Greg. "Just a few more minutes."

Mike moved away. He sat next to Dean. "OK. We are the salesmen. Let's make a list of companies we can visit to try and get some customers."

"OK," said Dean. "Let's start with the small companies. When we are used to working for smaller companies, we can try the bigger companies. I think most of the companies in the town use Harper's Design and Printing. Our prices are the same as theirs, but our quality is going to be better!"

"Yes," said Mike. "Our quality is going to be the best in the area!"

By 5:00pm, everyone was tired. Mike and Dean had made a long list of companies to visit. Dean planned to go to the places that had good access for wheelchairs. Greg had finished installing the software and setting up the computers. Jonathan had finished installing the cameras, and was helping Abeni to print the flyers.

"OK everyone," said Mike. "It's time to go home. Some days, we will have to work late, but we worked hard today. I think we should go home early."

"Why don't we all go to the pub to celebrate our first working day?" said Dean.

"Good idea!" said Abeni. "I don't feel like cooking tonight. We can eat in the pub."

"OK," said Mike. "Does everyone want to do that?"

Everyone nodded.

"Let's go," said Mike. "It won't be so busy now."

They set the alarm, and left the office. Jonathan locked the door. He looked at his smartphone. "Look," he said. "I can watch the inside and outside of the office on my phone."

Everyone looked at his phone.

"That's great Jonathan," said Mike. "Our office is safe with you!"

The workers enjoyed dinner in the pub. They talked about their future and their plans for the company.

"I want to make our company the biggest and best in the area," said Mike.

"Let's do it!" said Abeni. "We can be the best in the country!"

Everyone laughed. "That might be a bit difficult, but let's start by making our company better than Harper's Design and Printing," said Dean.

"We can do that, I'm sure," said Mike. He smiled.

Everything is going well, he thought. *Now we have to find some customers!*

CHAPTER SEVEN

Mike was tired. He looked at the time. It was 1:00pm. He had been going to businesses in the town to hand out flyers and his business card since 9:00am. Some people were friendly and interested in his business. They took his flyer and business card. Other people said, "No, thank you. We use Harper's".

I'll go to one more shop and then have lunch, he thought. *He went into a small women's clothes shop.*

The woman in the shop smiled. "Good afternoon, can I help you?" she asked.

"Good afternoon. I work for Artistic Design and Printing. We are a new company. We just started this week."

"Oh, I saw you on TV. You worked in the place that the government closed, didn't you?"

Mike smiled. "Yes, that's right. A few of us decided to start our own business."

"That's great!" said the woman. "I'm Shannon. I'll do everything I can to help you."

"Thank you!" said Mike. He looked at Shannon. She had long black hair and her clothes were very smart. She was wearing a suit. *She's beautiful,* he thought. *I wonder how old she is. Maybe thirty-five?*

Shannon looked at the flyer. "I usually use Harper's for my flyers, but from now on, I'll use you. What are your prices like?"

"The same as Harper's," said Mike. "But our quality is better!"

Shannon laughed. "You are a good salesman! What's your name?"

"Sorry, I didn't give you my business card. I'm Mike." He gave

Shannon his card.

Shannon shook his hand. "Nice to meet you, Mike," she said. "I'm going to have a summer sale in a few weeks. I need flyers for the sale. Can you do them?"

"Of course!" said Mike. *Yes! Our first customer!* he thought.

"OK, I'll send you all the details by email. I need the flyers this month. Is that OK?"

"Sure. We can do that," said Mike. "When we have finished printing them, we will bring them to you."

"Great service!" said Shannon. "I think your business is great. I'll tell all my friends to use your company. Many of my friends have companies. I'm sure they will ask you to do work for them."

"Thank you so much!" said Mike. "I really appreciate your help."

"No problem," said Shannon. "I want to help you. So, how many workers do you have?"

Mike and Shannon chatted about the business, and about Shannon's shop for a long time. When Mike left the shop, it was 2:00pm.

We talked for a long time, he thought. *Shannon is so nice. I'll send everyone a message and tell them we have our first customer!*

Mike sent a message, and soon he got replies.

---- *'Well done!'*----

---- *'Congratulations!'*----

---- *'Now we have a real business!'*----

Mike went to Julie's café. It wasn't busy.

"Mike, how is everything?" asked Julie.

"Good! I just got my first customer!" said Mike.

"That's great! And now you have your second," said Julie. "I want new business cards."

"Sure! Just send me the information by email," said Mike. He gave Julie his business card.

Julie took the card. "Thanks," she said.

"I'm tired and hungry," said Mike. "It's time to eat, and drink some coffee!"

CHAPTER EIGHT

Two months later, Ian and Paul Harper were sitting in their office, looking at the computer. They were looking at the website for Artistic Design and Printing. They were also looking at Twitter and Instagram on their phones. Many people were talking about Artistic Design and Printing on Twitter. The company had an Instagram account. They posted pictures of their designs. Ian and Paul were surprised. The designs were good.

"They have taken many of our customers," said Ian to his brother. "First it was Shannon in the clothes shop, then it was Julie in the café. Now, many businesses in the town are using them, and not us."

"They have stolen our customers!" said Paul. He was angry. "What are we going to do?"

"I don't know," said Ian. "Maybe we could lower our prices."

"No," said Paul. "We can't do that. I don't think people are thinking about the price. They are thinking about the designs. Their designs are better than ours."

"Our father started this business thirty years ago. Since then, we have been successful. This is the first time for us to lose money," said Ian. "We have to do something."

"Yes," said Paul slowly. "We have to do something."

Later that night, Paul met one of his friends in the pub. His friend's name was Jeff. He was a bad man. He had been in prison for fighting. Paul had known him since he was at school. They were sitting in a corner of the pub away from other people. No one could hear their conversation. They were drinking beer.

"I want to ask you something," said Paul. "I have a job for you."

"OK, but it won't be cheap," said Jeff.

"I know," said Paul. "Don't worry. I'll pay you."

"What do you want me to do?" asked Jeff.

"There is a new company in town. Artistic Design and Printing. It is run by a group of disabled people."

"Ah yes. The disabled people who lost their jobs," said Jeff. "What's the problem?"

"They are taking our business. We are losing money. Their designs are better than ours."

Jeff laughed. "You have competition! You should make your designs better!"

Paul didn't laugh. "There's another problem. People in the town feel sorry for them because they lost their jobs. They want to give them a chance."

"I can understand that," said Jeff. He drank some beer. "So what do you want me to do?"

"I want you to stop their business," said Paul quietly.

"Stop their business? How do you want me to do that?" asked Jeff.

"Maybe you can break into their office and destroy their equipment. They won't be able to work. Many customers will be angry. The customers will come back to us."

"OK," said Jeff slowly. "You want me to destroy their equipment. I can do that. But do they have cameras? A security system? An alarm?"

"I don't think so," said Paul. "I drove past their office the other day. I didn't see any cameras outside. But if they have an alarm, it's OK. You can stop the alarm, right?"

"Sure," said Jeff. "I'm a professional! But how much will you pay me?"

"Five hundred pounds?" said Paul.

Jeff shook his head. "Sorry, that's too low,"

"How about a thousand pounds?" asked Paul.

"It's still too low, but you are a friend," said Jeff. He shook Paul's hand. "OK, I'll do it. Don't worry. They won't have a business soon."

CHAPTER NINE

Jonathan was looking at his smartphone. He was watching the office while he was eating dinner. He watched the office most nights until he went to bed. He ate his pasta, washed up and then took his smartphone to the living room. He put the TV on, but he spent the night watching the office. At midnight, he decided to go to bed. He put his smartphone next to his bed, and went to sleep. He didn't see anything that happened.

Jeff was wearing a baseball cap. He looked at the time. 1:00am. There were no people around. There were no cars either. It was a dark night, and it was raining. The area around the Artistic Design and Printing office was quiet. He had a big hammer under his coat. He walked up to the entrance of the office and looked up.

There are no cameras, he thought. *Good. I don't think there will be cameras inside either.*

He took the hammer out and hit the door handle very hard. He hit it a few times, and the door opened. An alarm started ringing.

They have an alarm! he thought. *No problem. I can stop it.*

He went to the alarm box near the entrance and opened it with a screwdriver. He pulled the wires and the alarm stopped. It was very dark in the office, but there was a little light from outside. He looked around the ceiling. *There are no cameras,* he thought. *Good.*

He walked to the computers and smashed them with his hammer. Then, he went to the printing machines and smashed them. It took him fifteen minutes to break everything.

He smiled. *A thousand pounds for fifteen minutes' work. Not bad,* he thought.

He put the hammer back under his coat and walked out of the building.

The next morning, Mike, Dean, Abeni, Greg and Jonathan got a shock. They looked around the office. Everything was broken.

"I thought you watched the office on your smartphone," said Greg to Jonathan.

"I do, but I went to bed at midnight. This happened after midnight," said Jonathan. "But the good news is that we can see everything, because the cameras record everything."

"Let's call the police," said Mike. "Jonathan, try and find the data from last night."

"I can do that easily," said Jonathan.

Fifteen minutes later, two policewomen arrived.

"Do you have cameras?" asked one of the policewomen.

"Yes, very small ones," said Jonathan excitedly. "They are so small that the criminal didn't see them. I found the data. Look!"

He showed the policewomen the recording on his phone. The policewomen watched the video.

"Wait a minute," said one of the policewomen. "I know that face. That's Jeff Frodsham. He got out of prison a few months ago."

"But why did he destroy our equipment?" asked Mike. "I don't understand."

"Do you have any enemies?" asked one of the policewomen.

"No, I don't think so," said Mike.

"Yes, I think we do," said Jonathan. "We have taken a lot of work from Harper's. I think the owners of Harper's asked Jeff to do this."

"But we have no proof," said Mike.

"No, but we can arrest Jeff and ask him," said one of the policewomen. "If he doesn't tell us why he did this, he will go back to prison for a long time."

"He will talk," said the other policewoman.

"OK, you can arrest Jeff and find out why he did this," said Abeni. "But what are we going to do? We have no equipment. And we have customers waiting for their flyers and catalogues and business cards. We can't do our jobs."

"We have to call our customers and tell them about this," said

Mike. "I'm sure they will understand."

"Let's call the TV station and the newspaper," said Dean. "Then everyone will know about it."

"Good idea," said Mike.

"But how are we going to replace the equipment?" asked Abeni. "Does our insurance cover it?"

"No," said Mike. "We only have cheap insurance. It covers fire, water damage, and theft, but not this."

"We don't have enough money to buy new equipment," said Abeni.

"No," said Greg. "We don't have much money."

"We'll think of something," said Mike. "Don't worry. Our business won't fail."

That morning, a TV reporter and cameraman came. They filmed the office and spoke to Mike. A newspaper reporter also came. He took photographs and spoke to all the members of the company. Abeni posted the news on Twitter.

A few hours later, Shannon came to the office.

"Hi, Shannon," said Mike.

Shannon hurried to Mike.

"Are you OK?" she asked.

Mike smiled. "Yes, I'm OK, thanks. Just shocked."

"I saw the news about this on Twitter," said Shannon. "This is terrible! Who did this?"

"A man called Jeff," said Jonathan. "We caught him on my security cameras. I think the Harper brothers asked him to do this."

Shannon looked up at the ceiling. "Where are your cameras?" she asked.

"They are very small," said Jonathan proudly. "No one can see them.'"

"It's good that you found the criminal," said Shannon. "But what are you going to do?"

"We don't know," said Mike. "We are still in shock."

"Do you have insurance?" asked Shannon.

"Yes, but not for this," said Mike.

Shannon thought for a few minutes.

Then, she said, "I have an idea. I'm going to set up a crowd-funding page for you. People will read your story, and give you money."

"Great idea!" said Mike. "I didn't think of that."

"But how much money will we get?" asked Dean.

"I think you will get a lot of money. I think people will want to help you. Many people in the town were angry when the government closed your office. Don't worry." She touched Mike's arm. "Leave it to me."

Mike smiled at her. "You are so kind, Shannon," he said.

Shannon smiled. "I want to help you," she said. "I'm going to do my best. And I'm going to tell people not to use Harper's!"

CHAPTER TEN

The two policewomen parked their car outside Harper's Design and Printing. Ian looked up.

"The police are here," he said to Paul. "What do they want? Maybe they want us to do some work for them."

Paul looked out of the window. *Oh no,* he thought. *Did the police catch Jeff? Did Jeff tell them about me?*

The policewomen walked into the office.

"Good afternoon," said Ian, smiling. "How can I help you?"

"We'd like to speak to Paul Harper," said one of the policewomen.

"I'm Paul Harper," said Paul. "What can I do for you?"

"Do you know Jeff Frodsham?" asked one of the policewomen.

Paul's face turned red. "Er....er...."

"Well? Do you?" asked the other policewoman.

"Er, yes. We went to school together. Why?" said Paul.

"We arrested him a few hours ago. He broke into a printing company and damaged the equipment."

"Oh, that's, er... that's terrible," said Paul. He started to sweat.

Ian looked at him, then at the policewomen. "Why are you telling us this?" he asked.

"Because Jeff Frodsham told us that Paul Harper asked him to stop Artistic Design and Printing. He plans to give him a thousand pounds."

Ian looked at Paul. "Is this true?" he asked.

Paul sat in a chair and looked at the floor. "Yes," he said quietly. "We had to do something. The other company is taking all of our customers. I just wanted to help our company."

"You are both coming to the police station," said one of the policewomen. You can tell us all the details there."

Ian and Paul stood up and followed the policewomen out of the office.

The news about the damage spread very quickly. It was on the local TV news, and in the newspaper the next day. Shannon was interviewed on TV. She said, 'I have set up a crowd-funding page. Everyone, please help this business. They work so hard.'

Many people visited the office. They said, 'We support you. We are going to help you.' The next day the news about the Harper brothers was on TV.

"See!" said Jonathan, smiling. "I was right! The Harper brothers asked Jeff to stop our business!"

Many people in the town were angry. They contacted Artistic Design and Printing. They said, 'We used Harper's, but now we will use you when you get your new equipment.'

A few days later, Harper's Design and Printing closed. Shannon came into the office. She was excited.

"I checked your crowd-funding page!" she said. "You have over twenty thousand pounds! You can buy new equipment! And Harper's Design and Printing has closed. So now, you are the only design and printing company in the town. Everyone will come to you!"

Mike smiled. "Shannon, you are great. Thank you so much for setting up the crowd-funding page. And thank you for your support. We had some phone calls from some of your friends. They want us to work for them."

Shannon smiled. "You're welcome!" she said.

CHAPTER ELEVEN

A few days later, the new equipment arrived.

"Wow, look at this," said Abeni. She was looking at the new printer. "This is great."

"These computers are good too," said Greg. "I will install the software, and then we can use them."

Dean and Mike were looking at the emails on Mike's phone. "We have so many jobs!" said Dean. "Maybe we need to hire a new person. There is too much work for five people."

"Good idea," said Mike. "Maybe one of our old co-workers from Sunrise wants to work for us."

"How about Jill?" said Abeni. "She goes to the hospital often, but she can work part-time. And she is a good worker."

"Yes, Jill will be good," said Mike. "I'll call her now."

Mike called Jill. She was very happy to hear from him.

"Of course I'd like to work with you!" she said. "Can I start tomorrow?"

"Sure," said Mike.

"OK, we have a new member!" said Mike when he had finished the phone call. "Jill is starting tomorrow!"

"Great!" said everyone. "We should have a welcome party!"

"OK, I'm going to see Shannon," said Mike. "She is having another sale, and she wants flyers. I want to talk to her about the design."

Dean and Abeni looked at each other. "Are you sure that's why you want to go and see Shannon?" asked Dean.

Mike's face turned red. "Yes, what do you mean?"

Abeni laughed. "Your face is red," she said. "I think you like Shannon!"

Mike laughed and picked up his bag and car keys. "See you later!" he said, and left the building.

Mike drove to the town centre and parked in the car park. He went to Shannon's shop. There were some customers in the shop, so he waited until they had gone.

"Hi, Mike," said Shannon. "I want to talk about the design of the new flyer, but I'm busy today."

"Oh, sorry, I should have called you first," said Mike. "I'll come back on another day."

"No, wait." Shannon walked over to him. "How about we go out for dinner? We can talk about the design while we eat some nice food and have some drinks."

Mike smiled. "Are you inviting me out on a date?" he asked.

Shannon's face turned red. "Yes," she said. "I think I am!"

THANK YOU

Thank you for reading Let's Do It! (Word count: 7,526) We hope you enjoyed it.

If you would like to read more graded readers, please visit our website http://www.italkyoutalk.com

Other Level 3 graded readers include
A Dangerous Weekend
A Holiday to Remember
Akiko and Amy Part 1
Akiko and Amy Part 2
Akiko and Amy Part 3
Be My Valentine
Different Seas
Enjoy Your Business Trip
Enjoy Your Homestay
I'm Late!
I Need a Friend
Lincoln Takes a Trip
Match Day
Old Jack's Ghost Stories from England (1)
Old Jack's Ghost Stories from England (2)
Old Jack's Ghost Stories from Ireland
Old Jack's Ghost Stories from Japan

Old Jack's Ghost Stories from Scotland
Old Jack's Ghost Stories from Wales
Party Time!
Pretty and Bright
Roger's Long Ride
Rona
Stories for Christmas
Summer Days
The Curse
The Diary
Time to Go
Together Again
Who is Holly?
Wintertime

ABOUT THE AUTHOR

I Talk You Talk Press is an award-winning Japan-based publisher of language textbooks, graded readers and language learning/teaching resources. We won the Language Learner Literature Award in 2019 and 2020.

Our team is made up of highly experienced language teachers and translators, who have all studied at least one additional language to an advanced level.

This experience enables us to design our materials from the perspective of both the teacher and the learner. We consult with both teachers and language learners when designing our textbooks and graded readers, and test our materials extensively in the classroom before publication.

We are a fast-growing press, and currently publish graded readers for learners of English. We publish new graded readers monthly.